what we call civilization is relatively recent indeed, with the first permanent settlements occurring in the Middle East a scant 12,000 years ago. But the written record of our species' existence extends back only half this long, to the time humans invented writing and first farmed with animal-driven plows some 5,000 years B.P.

Sociology came into being in the wake of the many changes to society wrought by the Industrial Revolution over the last few centuries—just the blink of an eye in evolutionary perspective. The lower time line provides a close-up look at the events and trends that have defined **The Modern Era**, most of which are discussed in this text. Innovations in technology are charted in the beige panel below the line and provide a useful backdrop for viewing the milestones of social progress highlighted in the blue panel above the line. Major contributions to the development of sociological thought are traced along the very bottom of this time line.

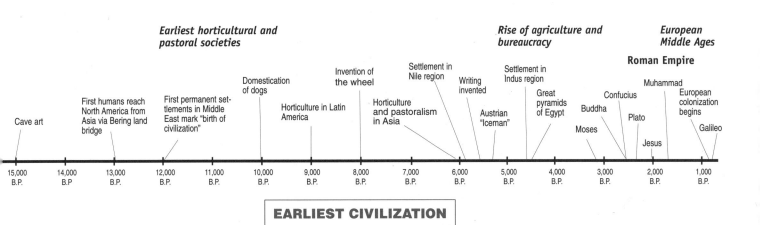

EARLIEST CIVILIZATION

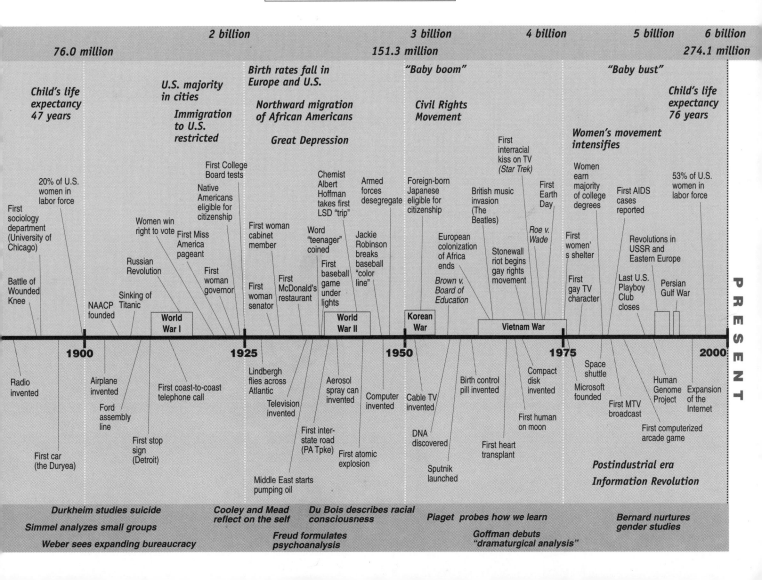

ABOUT THE COVER

People say you should never judge a book by its cover. In this case, however, go right ahead! Our cover captures sociology's basic insight about society: To understand our own lives, we must learn more about the society around us. The art in the center of the cover is a painting by Roger Bissiere titled *The Forest*. Looking closely at the painting, you can see a number of different individuals—the "trees"—engaged in their daily routines. It is easy to imagine that, as they go about their business, these individuals think mostly of their personal needs and concerns. What sociology offers is a new perspective that lets us step back from our personal lives so that we can see "the forest through the trees" and come to understand how society shapes our personal experiences.

The surrounding design says even more about sociology and what you can expect from this book. First, our approach is global—symbolized by the sphere at the top—with the goal of showing how and why people around the world have such different lives. Second, our approach highlights social diversity throughout the text, symbolized not only by the variety of people in the painting, but also by the way the surrounding cover is divided into levels from top to bottom. In other words, society involves not just difference but inequality because some people have far more opportunities and privileges than others. Third, taken as a whole, the design unmistakably suggests a computer chip, symbolizing yet another central theme of the text—the rapid spread of new information technology that is reshaping our social world.

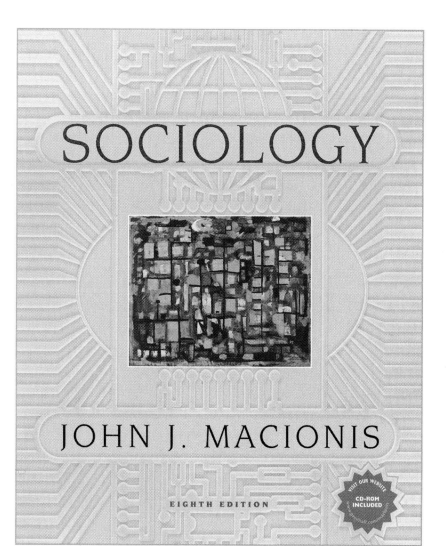

SOCIOLOGY

JOHN J. MACIONIS

EIGHTH EDITION

VISIT OUR WEBSITE
CD-ROM
INCLUDED

*This book is offered to teachers of sociology
in the hope that it will help our students
understand their place in today's society
and, more broadly, in tomorrow's world.*

John J. Macionis